About the Author

Sandy Day is the author of *Fred's Funeral*. She graduated from Glendon College, York University, with a degree in English Literature sometime in the last century. Sandy spends her summers in Jackson's Point, Ontario on the shore of Lake Simcoe. She winters nearby in Sutton, by the Black River. Sandy is a trained facilitator for the Toronto Writers Collective's creative writing workshops. She is a developmental editor and book coach.

www.sandyday.ca

ISBN-13: 978-1981942503
ISBN-1981942505

Copyright © Sandy Day 2011, 2018

All rights reserved. No part of this book may be used or reproduced in any manner whatsoever without the prior written permission of the author, except in the case of brief quotations embodied in reviews.

Cover design by Sandy Day
Illustration by Alexandra Plamadeala
Author Photo credit: Tony Hicks

Foreword to the Second Edition

The prose concordance that accompanied the poems in the original edition of Chatterbox has been removed. The author has divided the Chatterbox poems into four sections. A few poems have been added and a few poems have been removed. An index of poems is included in the end matter.

Chatterbox

Sandy Day

Chattering

Chattering

Born with this big bundle, bursting and chattering,
scattering love like dropped petals from wildflowers,
carelessly and carefully.

"Look what I picked for you, mommy!"
From my hot and sweaty hand she takes them, but later I
find them withered on the sand.

But still I am alive with love. Its pulsing, sensate, radiance.
Never sure it's wanted, wasted, welcome.

She tells me my love's too big to sit on her lap without
breaking her knees; her arms won't reach 'round it.

My love in me is flowing. You squeeze my shoulder and I
turn to see your eyes, so dark, so glowing, your smile,
knowing.

I love you, and it settles, smoulders like a smoky fume. I
love you and it flares; my kindling charred and crackling,
consumed in moments.

I love you, and I'm lost in it. Inside me, outside me,
flowing like a lifeline.

Hang on. I pull you out from drowning. I warm you up
and set you breathing.

I love you in. I love you out. Teeth chattering.

Baby Zombie

I am trapped. Can't escape. Banished to the cellar steps.
Examining my shoes through my tears.
Living in this house, moving room to room, unnoticed,
singing behind the curtains, floating in the bath. I am a
baby zombie, undead, bumping into walls, while
everyone, whistling, goes about their day.

How can I know what I missed if I never knew it was
missing?
My heart knows.

I am broken. Need a doll doctor to sew me up, clean these
eyes, bend back my leg. And walk out the door and keep
on walking til this house is far behind.

But I am trapped by the fear there is nowhere but here.

Chew my arm off instead.

Snap Shot

I am that little girl still. I am her.

The light shines on my head but I hear a thousand and one
questions unasked.

Why'd you stop loving me?

The tears pop.

I am that little girl praying for salvation. A hand, just a
hand, in mine.

This dead rat in my chest makes it impossible to easily
breathe but breathe I do around the rotten fur.

Grown up and perfect, knowing now.
This is not my rat.

Mercy

I walk the mile to her house in the summer furnace, the sun licking my shoulders. A heat keeps the dog low to the ground, following me in faith this walk will end somewhere.

I talk to God along the way, the buzzing tree toads, and dusty trucks rumbling by, the breathless wind. I feel each heavy, sweating step. My shoes smoulder – my path to you.

At her house we sit barefoot on the lanai and sip iced tea. The shade is merciful. I try to tell her – "Mom, I'm changing." But she will not hear me. She speaks of lavender and naughty deer nibbling down the shoots.

The dog sleeps under my chair. Her trusting slumber, her heart panting. I'm close. I'm near. She's dreaming.

The road back is longer, later. But at the end the icy lake awaits. I dive in. Divine to be in God's watery arms of cooling mercy. The dog stands watching – her vigil on the dock, and waiting.

iPod

My mother is a Luddite and her old knees are locking up,
swollen not allowing her to kneel in praise, her hands in
earth while planting yet another hosta offering.

Her garden is glorious. I watch safely through the screen
door, the wasps chewing the lanai, the brown bunny
hopping in picturesque, hell-bent destruction of the
tenderest shoots.

Shoot me, mother. I cannot close down quick enough to
avoid the pain. My rebellion dogs strain at the leash. I
think I'm open to each possibility. Teach me and I will
learn and never stop this quenching thirst.

I inherit an iPod and stare at its buttonless baffling circles–

I lift the needle to the vinyl, play, and hear the Luddite's
song.

She's living here, and here, I swear.

Spinning

I have been spinning my poor-me's into gold for all the days I can recall. And using that gold to buy everything that I can hold. But I have more to spin more each night. Rumplestiltskin.

I stand in the rain wondering when you're going to show up? Cold, and soaked, with all this gold in my pocket. And I will only wait another hour or two then you can go and get your gold from some other soul.

To all you fools who didn't buy, my outrage is screaming from the tallest tower, naked and bullied and ashamed.

There. I told you. Now you know my name.

Croatia

"It's not the end of the world but you can see it from there," you said.

The Adriatic Sea opened in me and I filled with curiosity. But busy, I intended to sit down later like a mouse with c cheese and nibble this strange land this Croatia country.

But you left me standing on the shore of the end of the world and I feel the emptiness of opportunity when the world cracked open for just a moment before you slammed the door.

I set about busily sweeping the crumbs, keeping the mice away from what's become of me.

Cinderella

I stand alone for the first time. All my Cinderellaring
around, complete. Ashes swept, but not for me.

A button hole as wide as the ox's eyelid once sagged in
me, in my center, gaping and drooping.

And I stood smiling in the straw, lost and leg locked to the
spot where I'd been dropped.

Food was sparse and the empty bowls rattled. The mice
giggled as the cats grew thin.

And the wind swept in.

I never looked beyond the window, what was outside. I
sat transfixed by my own knees.

And on them found the crumbs imbedded, carelessly
forgotten, never enough to nourish me.

The End.

No ball. No party. No masquerade. Just me. And in my
rags I stand with pumpkins growing, the old cock
crowing, and the day dawns that I am me.

Nourishment

Day after day I nibble and sip, devour and chew, feel full, am ravenous, go looking for more. I do not question the process of hunger, consumption, satisfaction, assimilation, and desire again.

But this guilt I feel for a dose of love. Always wondering why the little bit I got yesterday is not enough for today?

Hostage

Tis to this candy house I lure you. Come inside, I'll feed you.

My oven's always cooking, hot and dry, the sticky thin windows crystallize.

And as you hunger I call you in to lie upon this little mat.

I lock the door. I banish sisters. I want you fat.

The Witch

What's this I feel? Two tiny hands upon my rump? A shove and I am cooking in my oven!

I only wanted to eat this child, enslave the other.

What of my freedom? I am blind. This candy house is sweeter to the eye than churning in the gut – and I am starving!

Dying. A smoke now. A stench above the rank sweet melting of my hopes.

Tis the only meal I crave.

This morsel would whet me.

I fill with bubbling juices which I thought dry. I'm cooking with my maker. His fingers sizzle my ashy frizz and I am writhing in a burning expiration. Prick me. Stick a fork in. I am done.

Hansel

So smart. Birds cannot eat stones. At least they don't prefer them to croutons and bread crumbs. I drop my trail and clutch my sister's hand. We will find our way back in the moonlight. "To where we are not wanted," she whispers.

But I don't want back into that cottage now. That stone hearth, cold, and blackened with the smoke of confusion; empty and chilling, the chairs hard-backed, and sunken.

We are lost. The world spins 'round us. This central fear like a sun blazing and radiating its harmful rays beneath my skin, messing up the fat cells in my skinny arm.

I extend this chicken bone to fool you. So smart to know what predators will devour to stay one step ahead on the psychopath.

I am every part of this edible story. The cage, the stupid father, the blind witch, the push into the oven, the waft of smoke—the bird in those tall trees, the chicken bone, the peppermint, and the moonlight, glowing.

Flock of Crows

They screech across the morning sky caw cawing, a
murder after some prowling daylight owl.

Reminds me I have not thought of Dad in days, who tore
me with his claws and pulled the entrails from my body
leaving me for dead when he wasn't busy golfing.

Alarm sounded, the crows scatter, black feathers ruffled,
the threat diverted.

And I am as safe now in my seldom thoughts as the lost
white ball in the rough.

Grief Poems

This rain storm behind my eyes tingles, stinging to my nose and lip. Several angry lashes at the window pane, quickly dripping.

A ways off, a close pressure drop, a distant darkness, silent thunder.

This rain threatening, ever on the horizon, never arriving, ditches drying. In my eyes, behind my eyes, I fear the flooding of forty days and forty nights adrift and treading.

Since this pen learned how to talk is how long I've been swimming.

Scattering

Fracture

It's not the sound of a nut cracking or a knuckle popping –
it's the aching of the violin chord, of the harmonica wail;
it's the bending the fingers backwards whine, the swell of
tears filling up the space behind my eyes; it's this yearning
echo pacing like a coyote in a cage; it's the cry of this child
in my soul, tugging at my sleeve, love me, love me, love
me. No.

Resentment Doll

I stand here naked as a doll. Flat chest, slippery white socks, legs locked. A tiny pee hole so the mould won't grow. My plastic eyelids fail to open both together and my hair sprouts from sprockets in my hollow head.

Pull my string, "How do I resent thee?" Let me count the ways. I resent you to the height and breadth and depth of me. For every crevice you failed to kiss and every wrinkle you failed to smooth.

You didn't love me! All those years I wasted and couldn't walk away. You selfishly and fiendishly manoeuvred 'round me, left me tippy and off-balance, the head on my neck spun 'round the wrong way. When it was so plain, so simple. But your fear, which you disguise as dumb-dumb, prevented you from loving me.

And I became this plastic girl, this hollow heartless plastic doll repeating the story of my ancestry with a loveless you.

And how I do resent thee!

Dolls walk away in tiny plastic shoes they hobble. I am gone. You scarcely notice. I raise my rigid arm and aim to poke you in the eye.

Hello Winter

The winter approaches. Colour falls from the trees. Soon the boughs will be barren outside my window. The light fades faster, the day is gone before I know it, and the candles want lighting. I carve a pumpkin, numbing my hands in frozen pulp. Stabbing eye holes and a maniacal grin. I light the jack-o-lantern and watch it giggle in the darkness, flickering and cooking its own brain.

A scarecrow comes to life. He stands before me, plaid shirt, cocked head. Makes me follow him into friendship with his sad stupid eyes, fools me down a long, long path.

While he's sleeping. I find the matches. Light his shoulder, watch it smoulder. Watch him blacken, curl up and, fry, Goodbye.

Hello Winter.

Silence

The long cold silent winter stretches out like a thin blanket on a loveless bed. I trust life is breathing – a barely beating heart in hidden leaves and sunken acorns, frigid bulbs. The silence menaces me. No birds, no dogs, no screen doors slamming. No ribald teenage calls at two in the morning from the bus stop across the way. No songs ringing out on six strings sung with laughter and too much red wine.

The sun colours the sky as it rises. The bleakness blushes and I am reminded this too shall pass. The patience taught by winter, cold but not frozen nor forgotten.

Words

I'm haunted by words I said yesterday. They won't let me
go. Promises, vows, intentions—blowing the curtains on a
windless night. But they're just the soul of a dead decision.

I'm afraid nothing is so simple. To fall in love is dead easy
but not simple. The ghost is numbing, dumbing,
humming.

And I board up the old house. The weeds will grow and
the ghost will stay. But I will go because my heart has
learned new words it is dying to say.

February Days

These February days I remember this light, this rain, this
sound of car tires on the slick streets – when I was in so
much pain and desperate, driving him to work each way,
calling him a hundred thousand times a day – frantic to
make amends, to change my ways, and have a chance to
love completely and be loved again.
And now, this epitaph, I say, "I don't regret anything."
And he says, "All I have is regret."
Which I will forgive, but never forget.

Trees

Do not wonder when will I break? A February wind
blowing through the open window is cool and fresh. In the
dark, God is out there, before the dawn, in the black
branches and the inky blue sky. I am soft, but I am not
weak, and right now, I am not even fragile.
The rain fell all night. The trees are sodden and the tiny
twigs at the tips of the branches are drunk with drops of
water, and nubby with buds of promise.

If it freezes today, and the wind picks up I expect to slide
down the sidewalk and see those skinny twigs strewn
across the dirty snow.

Much is said of trees, and written. Roots grow deeper,
trunks grow thicker around the middle and proliferate in
my poetry. I enjoy the roughness of the bark, the tightness
of the foothold in the crook of the branch, the pinecones
and needles and abandoned nests.

I am not breaking this time. I hear the chainsaws droning
in the distance but I am not afraid.

St. Valentine's Day

I drag him to La Vie en Rose. Talk to him about it on the phone, say, "You can pick your Valentine." I am purring.

We park the car, kids at home, freezing night, our breath like steam. I clutch his arm and we stamp across the lot in frigid wind. I say, wickedly, "Choose anything."

But as we approach the door, he points to a window poster—a young and lovely model clad in lingerie extraordinaire. and says, miserably, "Can you look like her?"

Christmas Day (following year)

No gift at all.

Yesterday

He asks me, "What went wrong?"

Today

I wonder, what took me so fucking long?

Not Listening

I'm lost and all the night sounds aren't helping. The wind howling and I must trust one voice. Single out one sound above all else and follow.
In the cacophony, I'm confused and lost but the voice is shouting, so strong so sure I'm sure it is the right one –
powerful and sensible and I think I promised to obey it?
Oh fuck!
I'm lost again.
Can't hear.
So many babies laughing, sirens singing, waves crashing, a train whistling in the night, my lonely longing. Control myself! Find that voice. Follow it simply, blindly, to my silent grave, regretting every step I'm taking.

Last Days

This month – thirty-one single days of slow torture. Why?
So I will flinch at every wound and wince at every bullet
and never, never forget this lesson?

The lesson that I can't look the other way when someone
shows me their weapons – their I-will-never-really-love-
you straight razor, their greedy gutting gun, their fearful
fretted firearm.

The battle raging on this hill, silent as soldiers run and fall.
A battleground, a fortress wall, a foxhole.

I've dreamt this scene a dozen times. I'm trapped near a
tank in the grove and can't get to the big safe Beach House
without the massacre of machine gun fire across the no
man's land, which is my own.

The money rain begins to fall. All the coin bashing in my
brains, smothered, mouth stuffed with thousands, fists of
dollars punching holes in walls and in my skull.

Can the Wednesday in the middle come soon enough?
And then the slow slide down the other side.

And all there is for me today is music's comfort, Dylan's
harp, and the slow passage of time to safety of a lesson
learned real good, real slow.

Garbage Day

Your head on this spear and now I search for a place to stash it.

Didn't mean to decapitate you, just a habit I have, oops.

I impaled it on the spiked fence around my new home but my senses returned and I realized it will only attract birds and keep the children away.

Too bad it severed so completely; no chance for you to reconnect. Sorry 'bout that. Weak neck?

I'm sure your body still works. I left it by the old stump.

And blood stains – they're hardly noticeable on a man like you.

I swear, in the future, I shall control myself.

Ah, a trash. Just pop it in. Not recyclable, I think, but who knows? Let the worms decide.

Not Listening Again

You yell in my ear. Your blathering stack of cue cards and every stupid thought which enters your thick and foggy brain. Dumb words like swollen rotten food, bloated possums hang, can't you see I don't care? I've heard enough of this superficial hyperbole like a record skipping on the same insipid chorus heard it all before.

My heart is cold and shut up! Go away. Stop snoring in my bed. Get the fuck out of my head. If you awaken from the dead and your voice quietens to a whisper of humility or sorrow or regret, then I will listen, maybe.

Business

I'm gonna take fear out back and shoot him. Stand him up against the shed and blow his fucken head off. See his brains scatter, gritty and grey, like a cremated body. I'm so sick of fear. Want a divorce from this decrepit old man. Sick of listening to him, waking with him, feeding him, and tucking him in at night.

Courage is not the absence of fear, but moving on, dragging fear along behind. So, maybe courage is the creak of the rocker on the porch, which continues even as the wind blows, or when I sit to contemplate what's what? If I keep one toe to the floor boards, courage creaks as I rock.

The mound of earth by the shed, which worries the dog ain't my business anymore.

A Dead and Dying Dog

Still vicious, curled up in rigid death pose, tail bent under like a boney whip.

I back away, no sudden moves. I see the blue below his beady eye. He's still alive, and watching.

Those razor teeth, that whiskered jowl; any minute one last lunge and I am flying fur and mewling.

To think, he licked me, not long ago. Exposed, I choke my fear. Quiet, quiet, back away. In my throat, no noise, no purr. His ears twitch. He hears!

Freeze!

Still as a snail. Listen to the night, the death watch. Wait for his eyes to shut. Nine lives to ten.

Where, oh where is that tree?

Shallow End

He stays near the shore, skipping stones like forgotten
anniversaries. The fish at this depth are small and swim in
frantic schools with very little to say from their tiny
mouths. Too small to catch, too useless to eat.

The shallow water is safe; takes great effort to drown here.
And the sun beats down, tanning shoulders and knees to a
shoreline glow. The scene seems grand, like a postcard
from a summer long ago. But the stones are slippery on
the bottom and the night turns the water black here too.

The sand crunches under the foot step. Who wears their
shoes on the beach? An ominous sound — a man walking
on the beach in the night.

Nothing at this depth is worth fishing for.

Undertow

The tide is turning and in the draw the green frothy murk
of the undertow. I see the flotsam of his needs, scattered.
The sad rotting angels swirling, the helpmeet dying, the
precious words decaying – what am I saying?!

It's pulling – the setting sun and dragging love, backwards
down. I'm finding my warped and silty dreams, not
drowned.

This mess, this murkiness, dark becomes clear. I know but
I fight, there's nothing for me here.

I call the lifeguard. Down her ladder climbs her red and
white help. A clap on my heart. A blow to my head.

The desire and fervor washed away far. The sinking
dreams, the dithering star. And I'm not blaming – there's
no moon now. And the water swirls round in the
undertow.

Full Moon Coming

I almost dread this full moon coming. Full moons in June
are my undoing. They've glown above the lake's blue
gloom, and taken me down, my heart's locked room.

Heartbreak beneath a full moon's June. I hate it. Dread it.
Hide it. Caught it. That dreadful longing, a heart
unmatched, a sob, a lump, an aching throat.

Your love, stone cold. Suspended in the glowing orb. I
miss your milky honey drops. My breasts alone. My hands
unheld. I want your head.

Sit by my side and watch the weep. This sweep of sadness-
joy and hopeless doom. This damnable gorgeous June full
moon.

Choices

Down the river Styx, in dark and dirty water, I watch the
waterlog float past, rolling over, stinking slick and black
with leeches trailing. I clutch these colourful and breathing
daisy hands. Watch Hell float by. I am sickened. The
barren heartless home, not a home – a death box, and my
daisies wilting. The bandages, stained brown with blood
humiliation, and angry grass blade snippings, jetsam, pale
eyes washed out, full of useless lying tears, fumbled
frantic fears.

Over there is a festival of music and smelly cherry pie and
popcorn and I hear a man's melodic guffaw and a woman
shaking out a pinwheel quilt, dazzling the sunshine,
fractured, tulip red barn sunflower polka dotted
happiness. I'm running to it. Slapping down my entrance
fee and scrambling to do up my denims. I see my daisies
dancing, little raindrops drying at the corners of their
petals. Life is flying, a flag snapping, a fiddle reeling a
glorious wail, a dog barking a laugh and laying her sweet
head on her paws.
Life is twirling, lights streaming in a love river. My eyes
blurring, because I'm crying from the diving in.

Summarizing

So angry. I turn on the beach. My foot in the give way of
pebbles by the shore, the crunch and squishing futility of
the foothold.

I am not the drowned kitten I saw floating so long ago –
That hot summer when the lake putrefied and the sun
held the wind open like a pizza oven door.

I remember his red t-shirt torn, the sleeves ripped right
out, his freckly shoulders round and bare and burning,
and the curling smile and the sweat that poured from him
as we copulated there and there and there.

Remember? The ash from his cigarette fell, his hands busy,
his eyes squinting, his deep inhale. Red hot, but he turned
pale and wrote my name on the tiles of the bathroom stall.

Cold fish in the cooler. The condensation of endless beers
leaving rings on the table. And the Shakespeare I learned
imprinted on my soul. And he could never catch the white
petals shaking from my tree in the evening breeze lying on
the university's shadowy lawn, the cold stone buildings
needing no A/C.

I'm switched off. And love lies dormant like a cough I
recognize when it returns to rack my body with a summer
cold.

Worm

At the core, I find you green and glutted, pale and numb.

I have eaten the same flesh, sucked down the same sweet nectar, munched happily and carefree; the sun in the sky in my eyes.

And now, revolted, I find that I shared this world with you.

Silent Treatment

I withdraw my words, bind my hands behind my back
and struggle through a hundred mornings waking up
remembering with tears begun anew. A hundred spring
and summer eves, the big and hazy moon, trying to forget
my dream of watching it with you. A hundred days until
you find the scrap you wrote my number on and you call
and there you are, not silent anymore.

My jaw hurts – it's not God's will; it is my own, to punish
you for how I feel.

The Punishment

I am not corrupt. I plead for love found; feels me up, a
wiggling giggling serpent's seed.

A sadness driven deep. An anvil falling, a dash and gash,
a dint and thudding, a given and deserving end in
nothing.

The timing quickens, flashing, mounting, mountains of
heart changes. A determined mind, a phallus straining,
lips licked and salivating, waiting.

At the doorway the sprinkling urge of pity me and tickling
tingling tears of kick me. So foolish, so bereft again, the
end in silliness and deadly serious castigation.

Tea Bag

I dump the old tea – the bag flops out and lies draining, a drowned mouse in the kitchen sink.

I leave it there. To spite him. Even though he's gone and cannot see me leave it there til 3 o'clock when I might pluck it and toss it into the garbage can he said was too tiny when I bought it.

He told me a tea bag in the sink is depraved.

But I never agreed. And now he's left me to write about this soggy cold reminder.

Free

I fantasized you'd die (idiotically, but painlessly). That was the only way I could see this thing would end, and your friend would show up at your funeral for me.

I thought if I closed the coffin, called the hearse, the bells of condemnation would start ringing for me and never stop; for I'd buried and destroyed you, and what is worse didn't occur to matter to me.

I signed a deal, carved my epitaph, dated and doomed, my tomb designed and paid for. Ashes to ashes plan – a steal at any price.

The devil is astonished – the document dissolving, shattered and scattered by idiot wind from your very mouth. And I look up from the putrid funeral sandwiches and see a choir of angels singing a song written just for me and I am free – disbelieving – I am free ,miraculously, I am free!

Dead Horse

I ride him miles and years past his glue factory. The flies buzz and his long stringy tail lies flattened.

When am I going to realize he's never going to change, charge, a saviour, gallant and virile, snorting between my outstretched legs and hungry pelvis?

He's dead. The ride is over. My flogging only whips me. The frenzied foam flies only from my raging mouth.

I'm digging a deep and dangerous hole. Roll him in. Let's bury him. And watch the roses grow.

Divorcée

I crawl from the empty cocoon casing. A grey and dead fuzzy shell of deathly want. I am a worm, a crawly blind and handless sufferer, squirming dry and barren on the world. The spin of godly spindles so thin and nurturing fell in warp and aborted noosing and it's a decrepit and deformed mummy's carcass from which I crawl.

No moth, no monarch, no flight. The moonlight wasted, the candle flame low and unmoving. The sputter could be spit from my disgusting brown lip. I do not know.

My heel grinds into a terra firma. I feel the breeze in my silver hair, a puff of God on my rosy cheek, a glint in my steely eye. My wings unfold, and I fly.

Last Whisker

How can it be? I strain to see and pluck and pull – futility
– I thumb the prickly little wire that pokes through again
each week, each hour, growing like a menopausal weed
upon my witch's chin.

And the old man, afraid and spent, fingers frail as chicken
bones, pulled down the shades, lost his stones, bid
goodbye, death by poverty, alack, alone.

And as I stroke my soft new chin in pleasant
contemplation, I feel no more the stubborn prick of days of
sin. My inner whore, delighted to be free and faithful,
gorges on gingerbread, little boys, and wild boar.

A Friend with Skin

walks in and I have forgotten how to say. The words fall
from my mouth like teeth punched out. "Touch me," he
says, "No, with your hands." But my fingers are blind and
broken raw from this demon keyboard.
"Drink this," he holds the glass and words dribble down
my chin. Tongue don't fit, just spit. My friend with skin
picks up the phone, calls home. I'm already laying down
and dying.

The Dam

A pool. A vast, still, manmade lake of unmoving, frigid
water. Forty-eight years of cold cold tears. Murky ice, can't
see my hand before my face. Muck on the bottom, dead,
lifeless. And God stands on the shore wringing His hands
for the swimmer lost beneath the surface of the motionless
pond.

The barrier breaks. Who knows how, or why? The water
gushes, cascading frothy with anger and disappointment.
Everything comes to life, clinging to rocks, as frantic
fearless bubbles plunge over the edge of this tall tall dam.

And everything changes. The source doesn't dry up, keeps
flowing. The wind blows, the trees grow, the birds sing,
the fish swim. And I come to play. And I mean to stay.
And God turns away, smiling.

Blameless

Following the breadcrumbs – a trail through the forest,
backwards – leaving Hansel at the cottage, locked,
starving in the cage. Not to my home and father but to a
clearing where the words are given – sifted like sugar
falling on my head. And a new awareness feeds my
direction.

I am not lost – wretched as I am, I'm found. And kneeling
alone I open my only pack to display what it is I've got
that he might, like candy, pick and choose.

Swiftly, he takes it all. Sweeps it up and in one gulp I am
devoured and absolved and taken truly by this hungry
God.

Craving

Rockabye

My path is blocked. A tree, grown wild and large. I cannot step around, its branches reach me, tickling me, poking me, its roots trip me as I try to pass. So I stop and look up into the leaves, shapes I don't recognize with these eyes.

The tree shakes down manna I have not tasted for a long, long time. I sit down to feast and laugh. Leaning up against the trunk, comforted and fed, the tree envelopes me, infuses me with a strange yearning desire.

As the moon rises and I sit chomping on an apple, I wonder, why this tree, God? Why now? For I can't sit here endlessly rubbing my hands up against this mossy bark, can I?
What reason, God, for this sojourn, this absolute barrier that I can't see around?

I am uncertain – to try and pass seems hopeless, to turn and walk away, just dumb. Am I to lay me down right here and die?

The tree is silent. And so is God. No instructions. I climb up and through the branches and the leaves I glimpse the sky beyond and trust, which is the hardest part, this bough won't break.

Abuse

The snake twirls up the branch. A winding slippery
embrace. His tongue flicks, his eyes aglint. I am a tiny
blonde child, fearful and paralyzed. A pomegranate
lodged near an Adam's apple sore.
His puzzling slithers. My little shorts snag on my hot
parts.

I am two eyebrows meeting. I am scalded by a forgotten
iron. I am hiding in the laundry basket. I am swallowed
half way.

Eden

I stand here munching on this apple with him, eye to
glittering eye. He's dangling from a branch, and we
continue our dialogue: "I don't really want to live forever,"
I muse. "But I'm finally finding my passion. And it's lovely
and wicked, just like you."
He smiles and hisses. Curls his thick body in flattered
delight.

"I told you, you wouldn't die," he says.

Now he's my saviour.
He planted his seed. And contrary to how the story reads,
no bruising enmity exists between him and me.

God knows everything. But lots of times, He's holding
back and scaring me!

The serpent crawls up into my belly with the apple. I am
dust without him tempting me.

Coming and Going

It oozes. Fresh! A slap, my blush. The offering, sweet, a
segment, dripping, innocent. My fingers, your tongue,
wind 'round my coming to this, no victim, leaving this,
hurting to the tubes, backing up in a mirror, a dripping,
the crazy.
The coming, the going, aloneness, aloneness, the
connection, the warp, the woof, the power cord ripping,
skin peeling and crawling, no ends to a snake sucking its
own tail.
Dripping, the venom, the semen. I'm empty and craving,
begging and begging!
This coming, this going.

Resolution

My lips shall not speak a resolution this year. Instead they will whisper a prayer, kiss a hand, press it to my cheek. Bereft and longing, but I cannot resolve a path—will not resolve a path.

I pick my way through the orchard, stepping over ancient fallen branches and rotting fruit corpses. The sun, sinking into the horizon, blinds me, though I see a tree in the distance, a silhouette, black and invisible, and I am pulled forward even as it disappears.

I say to Adam, "Get out of my way. You're blocking my view."

That tree mesmerizes me.

I hear my beating heart, a serpent hissing, a bird in laughter. Trust that God does not mock us.

Turn over the hand, kiss the palm, let it happen without resolution.

Status Quo

A fiction of the mind? I am such a story teller with characters so thick and sick and plots so never-ending and pathetic? I cling to these decrepit notions like a slimy gull-poop-covered raft adrift in a putrid lovesick ocean?

On better days, when the book lies splayed and forgotten in the corner where I've thrown her (this naughty dirty daughter), I move with a humming buzz and zing emanating from acceptance – a blank and wondrous thing. On these days I know I'm meant to write and watch from the back row (and maybe not watch at all, maybe close my eyes and kiss you long and slow).

Clementine

I peel a Clementine and contemplate the world. My world.
Soft little peel spongy, barely clinging to the fruit gives
way like a thin chemise. He handed me this orange, so
perfect and round, absolutely quenching, sweet and
bursting in my mouth.

The sky storms. Winter falls. The sun obscured by a
million miles of frozen tears.
I know what I want. What my heart wants. The lingering
bitterness of citrus on my fingers. Hungering for more of
this magnificence, this sun in the palm of my hand.

Pray for wisdom. Fill me up.

Blooms

I am weighted down by the beauty of the full-blown bush.

Once upon a time, I grew a rose, but snipped its buds in their rolled and soft perfection.

I prefer the unbloomed rose before it opens and begins to drop its petals.

These bushes sag, burdened by their aging beauty. It is too much! And too plentiful for me to look upon too long.

I wonder of the mistress of this house, with her shiny parked Mercedes. She is secure enough and loved enough. She needs not risk the thorns, shears in hand and sweaty cotton gloves, to offer her own unfurled heart a clutch of roses?
And then, there are the peonies.

Little Prince

I weep for his friend, the flower, smothered under glass, and wonder, are her roots withering?

Roots. So ugly, their spindly tangle, a hidden beauty, the toppled tree, the accidental bulb in my hand torn as I weed blindly in the garden.

The carrot of a dandelion, the shallow sand beneath the spruce. I brush and shuffle, shake off this rush, this insistent bud, and flower before my time while trimming my thorns.

The Apple Tree

Gnarled old thing with twisted limbs and thick grey bark.

I lean on the fence watching as birds fly in, disappear into the leaves, reappear flustered, flutter off drunkenly.

The fruit glows dark and shining like eyes across a room. I wonder, for I've ate apples sweet and new but I've picked apples wormy and dry.

Such a divine old tree. Somehow so familiar.

This fence is falling down.

Bad Timing*

You slip into my life at just the right moment. Send me spiraling into a dimension I'd forgotten or found, I can't remember. And now I understand the waning and the waxing, the changes and the passing, the brilliance and the darkness is nothing I said. Nothing I do effects the moon's passage.

I look up each night sky it looks down. Connecting. Stone to eye, blamelessly rising, *a fallacy, eclipsed.

Creamsicle

I know this is the delicious part, like the sweet ice-cream
'neath the tangy orange dip, before the stick (wooden and
stale, which my teeth need to chew).

So I savour this part –

like a hot summer day, soaking up sun, my toes in the cool
lake, stickiness on my fingers and tongue.

Just saying, love's awesome!

Salt & Pepper

We match like a set. A slight difference, the hand detects
as it reaches for a dash of seasoning. But matching – meant
to stand next – lonely if the other breaks, bereft, and
pairless.

The Collector finds us, dusty and alone, at separate
Church bazaars and cries, Eureka! Sets us together at His
feast.

And I am shaken. This sweat , these tears, crystallizing.
These years of searching, ending in my match, my
sombrero, my windmill, my ceramic heart, stops breaking.

Candy Man

I eat you, candy man. Don't think I don't. I start at your
voice and sniff your vibrating vocal chords, and then your
hands—I chew each finger to the bone. And then your
eyes I keep them in my pocket for later.
And now your clothes fall from your back. I lick your skin.
I take you in. You're soft and chewy, no crunch at all,
sweet and hard for sucking a long long time. Your mouth ,
your tongue, your cock, I eat you up, candy man. Don't
think I don't.

Caged

The tiger paces back and forth, back and forth. She hears him growl, impatient. She stops to watch and he looks right at her, eyes locked on, mesmerizing. Transfixed, she thinks, he'd be so soft to touch, one touch, if only while he sleeps.
The cage, taller than a life of regrets, seems insurmountable. He looks to her so harmless, so inviting as though she could set him free, so he can eat her alive.

The Lyric in You

The lyric in you reaches inside me recalling volumes of
past gardens, fresh fig leaves I gathered, not inherited, free
from old arrow wounds in my hand.
I listen to you, this song you sing continuous to my soul I
am magnet to your homonyms, your conjuring of every
need I've ever known.
I collect your words in a philtre jar you keep spilling while
I sit under this Bodhi tree with you forever filling this lyric
willing.

Concupiscence

Now here's a word which rolls not off my tongue. My
tongue these days lies quiet, no longer licks my lips while
you describe the tightening of your bow.

And in the center, is that the flight of Cupid's arrow?

Ah, my tongue, which longs to know all measure of you,
slipping from my conscience and the consequences. My
tongue lies silent.

Waiting for the trilling and the thrilling which only your
tongue does to me.

Birds on a Roof

Love denied is written. Love thwarted is composed.
Lovers hidden sing the words which resonate forever.

If you took my waist and kissed me full where they could
see, after the squawking flap settles back their wings to
silence, I will not write.

I'll be too busy memorizing you.

Barn Fire

The slightest touch from you spreads the smile in me like fire thrilling along a path of dry grass from the controlled burn to the barn's door.

I imagine you and the farmer's wife inside your sensible brick house. You are shaving at the kitchen sink, she is yelling at the kids and peeling potatoes for breakfast.

Lay me down, listen to the cock crow, and care not for whom. The hay is soft, the scent divine, the fire smoulders, and you are mine.

Balls

I can't keep track of the moon. Last night it gleamed at me from straight above like a bald and brazen ball.

The clouds drew back their sexy curtains and it hung exposed and bold and fully attentive. Winking at me!

My astronomy acumen is out of orbit. I watch the house across the way stand still as the sun rises from its roof. My eyes fixed and locked, determined on daylight while my heart stays out wandering its midnight philandering.

To the Archer

His crooked arrow with heart shaped tip makes it easy for
me to fall in love, makes it easy for me to find his mouth
and want to hide my passion in it.

As the arrow flies, it fires through a bird instead, which
flutters to its death; an easy fall, a soft and feathered
thudding (that was my heart). Whispering, Oh God, Oh
God, did you hear it? Coming?

He puts away the bow and I am left, this empty quiver.
Where is that arrow? Find me alive again, pierce my soul.

Pressure

He is here as we band together. You pressing up against my side, my front , my back, my brain. And I slip into you and over you and onto you like a knot.
I hear the band. I see that band. I am banned. I hear church bells in a floating melody on summer air. He is here as our hearts band because we can, because we can't, and I recite and remember every word of the promise of your pressing.

The Daisy

Loves me, loves me not. A fickle prickly banter. Makes me laugh, hears me cry. I hold my breath, bite my lips, he begs for more. I lean to kiss, he walks away. I am adored.

No way to know. The petals fall, the daisy stalk is bald. He loves me not. I'm sure. It's cold.

I cannot wait. I grow insane. I crave the feel but hate the pain. Toss the daisy. Walk away. Die to live another day.

Maybe

Maybe I can't have you—and God weeps—maybe. And
my love for you wanders from you like a deflating balloon
on a long long ribbon, bouncing and tangling and bobbing
in the wind, away where different voices prompt me and
urge me and soothe me, where coffee cups and cake plates
clatter on different tables.

And I sigh an inward blind sigh always way back in my
mind – a puff, not enough to inflate another balloon –
remembering we never, we never, and I miss a you I never
knew, but wanted to.

Maybe I can't have you, ever. And I will know looking
backwards when this party hat slips and all my hoping
and wishing and blowing out candles is revealed for
naught.

I am staggered and humbled by your resistance. And the
prick of your pin on my skin.

Shh

Don't tell. I fell. This spell.

Can't breathe. Can't see. Hear your voice in my tea.

Like a wish, like a dream, all around, in my sleep. Save me.

Want you so bad. Feel sad. Can't have. Just pray. Can't say. Hear your touch all day.

Turn back. Antidote, long gone, long passed, no hope, all alone.

Fell fast. In deep. Feel cheap. Thirsty. Potion broke. I'm smoke. Lust now? Trust, how?

Can't breathe. Can't see. Hear your voice in me.

Honey from the Rock

I bend toward your mouth and kiss to last a thousand years. A golden liquid store and as it drips one sweet memory a day escapes. I memorize your eyes and lip and wish you could feel me crawling with silent velvet feet across your heart, and you would sting only me.

Fingers

This terrible joy, this exquisite pain, all at once like a
storm.

A part of my soul's secret flies with you and when I think
for a moment that you don't know it I forget all my lines
and stagger under the wasted passion and the missed
chance.

What happened here? How, in the dark, and with just our
fingers did we find each other?
My heart hurts thinking, my heart hurts remembering,
so my brain tries not to.

Sometimes stupid decisions are made by people at desks
with stiff shirts and thick wallets. And I will never
understand, but if you need me to, and disbelieving I let
go.
But you will never go—and I feel this terrible joy, this
exquisite pain.

Close

I came so close to love's sure shoulder – brushed by and
paused, looked eye to eye, and felt his fingers reach to
draw me closer for one brief moment as I passed by.

I registered the sigh – the secession in the touch, the cheek
to forehead press, goodbye, good luck, so briefly held but
abdicating much.

And later when the touch was resurrected, the subject of
the softness of my breasts, and thoughts emanating from
his chest, in lust, in such a span of time a spider could not
have fallen faster.

The shoulder is closer, the pause is longer, bone to thigh,
face to face, turns me around in my surrender. Propriety in
darker eyes and devotion's futile embrace.

Voyeur

Perspective is everything.

I look back, drag the past up to meet the future.

See the destruction. Watch a hundred hearts crumple and bust.

I see it now.

You taught me, parting my lips.

I speak it. You drew it. This truth is the ruin of you.

I brush the dust, the shards of desire and dirt of penance into a small pile.

We both need a spy glass to see that God is everything (just like perspective) or God is nothing

and I hear His voice but I no longer see.

Chicken

I cluck my fear to you and you rather tease me than cover
me with your wing. You call me from the stinky, dark
coop with your hard kernels and cocksure crowing. My
eye twirls, wondering how you withstand the wind which
scatters the seed through your cock and comb?

My feathers ruffle and I scratch but I'm never going to
crack your shell.

Nothing is more grisly than this betrayal I feed
myself.

Snap Dragon

Maybe I told you I'm strong – I'm not. I think one day you said I was a storm, a flower. I'm weak and wobbly, blossom too heavy, rain is crushing me.

I wish you could hear my heart, the flame crackling as the royal jelly bubbles. I am not strong and confident. My wit is accidental now. I'm hurt, smudged and tired, bending over in this storm, bending, breaking, snapping off at the dragon's tongue.

And Deliver Us from Evil

You are eating my soul like a fire licking the edges,
warming me, toasting me, a sweet sweet incense. You are
consuming me, burning up my truth, my harmony,
singeing my eyes with your sin. And your song burns me,
blackens me, destroys me, chokes up my throat.

I poke your heart, and it is ash.

Spellbound

I do not deserve this spell. At first it is my God who
reaches down His gentle hand and head and lets me
scramble up to hold Him.
He whispers stories in the night – I wake up writing,
crowing! Happy and delighted – my God has found me or
I Him, and let me in, let Him in, lay down and wrap my
arms and smell the divinity the nape of His neck is
issuing!

But then – like an endless bell, lowly tolling in my ear, I
notice you standing very near. And you tempt me with
candy and the sweetest whistle I will ever hear and a look
of pleading pleasing sympathy and a lust only wolves like
you can hide for moments at a time.

I trip and fall. Right at your feet, I fall. And when you
gently help me up you pour me tea, you very subtly and
sweetly honey baby – you poison me!

I'm bound upon this lumpy bed. My backbone broke, my
eyes blinded. My words fled and in their stead a fixation
on the closing door, your footsteps running past, away,
forever more.
Locked and paralyzed with grey hair growing, pots of
gold are overflowing but nothing, not a thing to buy or
spend – cock stop crowing!

My God does not abandon me. He watches the treachery.
And I feel hollow and so light like I could blow away, a
feather, a thistle, a sprite.

This terror, this poison, coursing through my blood, spilling, and I curse you your warmth, chilling, as I harden to a statue of bitter frightened abandoned spellbound Cuckoo!

Old Goat

Why do I battle this horny old goat? He turns me from my
God but not away. He turns me so he sees me from the
rump, the glinted slice in his eyes pulled back and
gleaming.

I find myself on my knees worshipping him. My
apprehension swallowed as his horns grow wild with
ejaculate suppressed.
He weakens me with fitful desire and ruttish sluttish
wanting.
I am in awe – this stag, his potency and plunder.

I can't make sense of this sudden coming, my
concupiscence unbridled when my thinning hand was on
the pasture gate.

But now my milky skin in luxuriant goat milk froths and
covers my delighted breasts in foam, this stone against my
lips invites him in to eat a fig and sip my nectar sweet

I lean on my God – he prods me as breathless I bathe in
gratitude. Giving up, giving up, restless in defeat.

Exit

I'm heading for the exit. All the lines are running through my mind. I hear a song but only the refrain and one voice singing, Aw!

My ego wants all exits blocked, all tickets torn, all trailers shown. No mystery, no candies rustling, no delicious waiting, no fingers searching for the prize.

Suspense and time suspended.

My exits, stacking up like the trash in the alley behind the door store, waiting to be hauled away, leaving nowhere.

Glowing red behind the curtains a simple word EXIT

but I don't want to go. Aw!

Cracker Jack

I get it. I get it. You're the prize, bric-a-brac, you're the
cheap piece of crap in the Cracker Jack!

When I am through with the sweet stuff and occasional
nut and picking the kernels from my teeth and clearing
my craw, I divine you, preserved, just for me, in plastic
wrap. And my sticky fingers eagerly undo you and we
play and we play til one day I notice, you're inanimate.

You drop from my life to the floor, a feeble clatter. Just like
that. My monkey, my prize, handing me my treasure back.

Never

I write and imagine you reading and not turning away in
disgust, "Ahh this chick, man, she won't leave me alone!"

You get on with life as I should too – Snap to attention,
forget all that stuff.

Twas nothing?

I must be impaired in the part of my brain which
processes holy connection.

I ask God. And in His wisdom He is silent, as I should be?

"I never tell you stop" you said one day. You said, never.

Pillow

The instruction to allow myself to write what is in my mind and thoughts unstopping, the permission plumped me.

And now, I silent sit, pen restless writing your name and your name and the pain and your turning away.

And every little minute, every bit and byte flutters around me, a burst pillow, a mess of tickly prickly softness and I am clouded and have nothing left to say or to lay my head on to dream.

Goodbye

I can't believe I say goodbye. A silent word I dared not speak to you. And last week if asked, or rather, forced, I would not find goodbye residing in my torso. But in my head the word stood in ready waiting to save its mistress.

Goodbye came unbidden. My attachment furious and forever or so I thought. The first verse is barely sung but I'm undone and see the goodbye in the chorus coming. Better to whisper it while I have strength, if only from my heart, because I wonder with my brain how you passed up the chance to take me down again?

Erato

You took her with you (as I scrape the pig fat from the pan and start to cry again). I know she's in your hands, you smoothing back her hair, whispering in her ear, her eyes igniting the words in you which once lit in me when we shared her.

My tears plop into the pots and dirty dishwater. I write nothing.

Missing you eats my entire heart and art escapes me. She drifts back to you from whence she came, Erato, doing dishes.

Spilt Ink

So much wasted. Pages and pages while you stored up my words like a pornographic stash and spilled them later over your own hand.

And the Divine—who sneaks into the thinnest line, flattened like a mouse, niggling and chewing and reminded me of the trespasses I must never mind – He is in my pen, writing me an adventure I see looking backwards, live moving forward, understand looking sideways. He rubs up against me in the night.

This spill trickling down my thigh, leaving a stain where you came, where you went, leaving all my pens empty and useless.

Pig

This word slops around, glances innocently, blinks with
long white lashes and small dismissive eyes, looks away.
Ignorance marks its flat flabby nose like a smear of green
manure it gruntingly doesn't know is there.

Your pristine illusion I sharply inhale this ammonia word,
pig. Pale, hairy testicles like water balloons sway and
cloven hooves in stilettos trot.

This word is a mistake I abhor, harmless and tasty when
sizzling on a fork but so heavy it rolls over and squashes
its own piglets.

I reach for your hot full cheek, tilt your face to mine, check
your lips, your eyes, for purity, and chastity, your spirit.

No, pig, no doubt.

Surgery

With no anaesthetic you pull out the sharpest blade and
swiftly cut, and my arm falls off.

Unarmed, I am surprised it's so silent — the bleeding
packed and only blooming when I move too much.

And there's no follow up. No reattaching that gangrenous
cold member.

Now I am left to grow another?

Wasted

The sadness started in my dream and I awoke in pink and orange and I can't love you!

Holding out this sphere and watching your head on the pillow, my fingers pulled apart the segments and put them to your lips and you consumed me, burning all of me a singed and curling love note blown away before I even read one word.

I'm useless in this longing, useless, a black smudge on fingertips. Praying to accept it, take this orange into my own mouth and feel it bursting, a pleasure, an agony, my squandered love, so close to telling you so you are tingling from the knowing you already tingle from, this pinkness, my smile, my everything mingling heart and mouth and I can't give it. Sphere falls, quenching out.

Red Light

The red light, the stop sign, I see it. Through the fog and rain and silence, I see it.

And all it is to me now is a hidden heart pleading. The tiny red hope in a tin man's chest bleeding.

Crucible

I miss you from the crucible which is my heart. Soft rosy petals crushed, a mush of bleeding in my hand. I miss you and you I long to know, the ascent peakless, a summit unclimbed. I miss you on my knees, connected and flowing, my prayers pleas for understanding.

I am an unbeliever, astonished, sorely amazed, that hearts like ours beat their rhythms so far apart that they are silent when I should have my ear pressed against your pounding chest.

I miss you in a part of me which only knows when it is loved but tenderly puts hope aside for wishing you are safe and home and missing me from the crucible where it began and sorry smoulders.

Knocking

Temple of God

The story begins with a woman lain open on a hillside, an archangel whispering an orgasm of shooting stars!

I see her lying, her long hair loose, her dark eyes wild. Opening her temple to Him not to offer herself but to gobble Him up and hold his love tight inside.

And so a child, conceived, her concession – a life of mother-pain, watching her son die of his Father's love, for his Father's love, if only once, if only for a moment. For His love.

Knock

I knock. Not knowing for what I hunger. Not bread nor stone, not fish nor serpent.

I asked, before. No answer, before. But now I knock and He answers. I seek and He finds me. I love and He loves me.

Somehow I know how to give good gifts and meekly ask. He thunders in response.

The law and the prophets say this is so. If I do to man what I most want man to do to me, my wish will be heard and answered. Do?

A fish, a stone, a tree, a bone. I knock and my life is opened.

Yes

I say yes to this gift, on my knees, fumbling for words, yes, yes, yes.

You want me this way, this madly? Then I am yours. And I say yes to this gift.

I didn't see to read. I couldn't find the lock. I wouldn't turn the key. I didn't hear what I could not say. It was there in my mouth, yes.

The light pours in, the early morning. A whisper wakes me. My first thought is of him, your prayer on my lips, lead us not into temptation, but deliver us from evil.

I say yes to this gift. This prickling, quenching, numbing, and humbling gift. I am blessed.

I say yes.

Since I Met You

A hundred poems. A notebook full. A heart torn open, no pages missing. Since I met you the planet shifted, the islands drifted, the tide pulling, my desire for you castaway and drowning, out to sea in choppy waters, no raft, no compass, no way home.

It is a pleasure on my knees to feel God's hand upon my head. My kisses 'round his navel, comforting and breathtaking to put out to sea with Him. But longing and lingering in the sadness of never knowing, never touching, since I met You.

A dark and stormy sky, an ever-changing ebb and flow of ink and paper see-you-later disappearing in the darkness and the undertow.

Sun

I care nothing for the sun – I barely glance, but its
reflection in the moon – night long I gaze at that.
The sun is like the older brother – I have no interest – he
burns too brash, he is too loud, too old, too proud.
The other days, when light is muted and shadows subtle,
stir my soul.

The sun, so powerful, bursting from its tent, cock naked
and crowing, heat seeking in one eyed confidence – and on
the ground, knees drawn, I turn away, but it touches my
hair and cheek, nudges me to play. Okay. Just for today.

Until it's gone again and I lie down to sleep.

The Difference

From the library I took two books. One of God poems, one
of love. And read them side by side each day and could
not see the difference.

O' that you would kiss me with the kisses of your mouth!
prays the solemn Sol.

Surely God is not some gentle reaper but a rapacious
rapper come knocking in the night – Yo, Muthafucka, this
a booty call!

I find God in delight – it's not like He sleeps nights!

Love is tailing me down the street, a bitch in heat, a dog
unleashed. Or is that God's purring and growling I heed? I
don't care he's catching me!

Poems do not belong in books. They read from groins and
every romance tongue. I am certain God is drunk and
singing in His creating both of one.

Eros Ascending:
A Book Review

I'm done this nasty book, its title exalted, its illustration
divine (Eros and Psyche in passion entwined). Tis nothing
but clap trap promising the stars, a prolonged orgasm
manual with a profound lack of God.

Love reaches into me the arm of God, straight through the
top of my head into my heart and for a few magic months
love fills everything I think and breathe and then it's gone.

Divinity is fleeting. To make my heart search, to imagine
the passion of my Christ and cry my tears for him dying.

Love is no rock star copulation, no blonde infatuation.
Love is the weariness of waking to a child's crying and
setting the dream I was dreaming quickly aside so I can
minister to God's child and my own – comfort, solace,
presence til he is grown.

What's missing from this book, which seems so plain, is
the notion of serving not yourself someday.

Love is not making love. Love is being present.

More?

I ask for delivery of a kind and passionate spirit. One to
touch me in the night and sing into my soul. I ask for what
I found but cannot hold.

And I ask for deliverance from my lonely will and fear.
Step back and watch my self pressing through this mirror.

I didn't know my heart was delivering until they told me
so, and now I ask the question, how did he ever let me go?

I ask for everything in return and have nothing left to give
– except my wish, my prayer, my love, in this whisper on
my lips.

Suffering

I step into the church and hear the creak (all churches creak), the pew, the floor, the door, the imperfection of the human structure, creaks in echoing emptiness.

I look up at the glass story, dazzling deep colours within a lancet arch, a story of suffering or ecstasy garbled with horses and saints, swords and laments, pulling my eyes up into God's.

Sitting shoulder to shoulder weeping, I am safe. Set free among the mourners, scrunching my tissue, the words drop into my body like thunder – Yea, though I walk through the valley of the shadow...

I hurt in a part as empty as a confessional, dark and unvisited by the likes of me. No one holds this holy relic. I rise (knees creaking just a little) and shuffle off to the hall, to funeral sandwiches and stand in awkward society, the moment with God, vanished, the sufferers chewing.

Sinners

Sitting among the sinners, I am at home. I love one who washes my feet, teaches me to lift my eyes and prayers higher than the desert stars in the darkest night.

A lost soul sleeps through the scene waiting for the dawn. Only moves when he can see. Trusts not my company.

The wine in this stone chalice turns to water as I drink. I thirst to learn the ridges and valleys of his Jerusalem, long to take those hands and hold them to my lips, my breasts, search those dark eyes, hear that voice, watch that tongue speak.

I look back to see the petals on the path where we crushed through the garden. I hear the stories told, the truths so bold, the laughter thrilling.

How does he lie by his sleeping cattle, knowing his disciple waits?

The trials are many, awesome foes and bloodied thorns, but gentle sleep is waiting. My bed too empty forever without him. Heart open, eyes lifted, prayers enter like love letters. I sit among the sinners, receiving.

Time

Suddenly I fill with time. All the time I could possibly
need. I jump from the waiting clear into the being and I
am timed with a filling I forget to measure in the living.

Hidden

Up in the blue, blue sky of this morning an orange moon is waning. I'm up so early I catch it before it turns to stone.

The moon reflecting fire, daring drawn from an unseen source.

I've been up for hours pondering your influence.

The Meeting Place

I see a giant's glove dangling from a tree branch like a
dead man.

And inside the church three Marys sit and share their
whispered wisdom, usually.

I wake up with that dead man hanging in my sleep—
moving in the breeze, dirty and sodden, leftover from
Hallowe'en?

Trudging down this street, a long and lonesome time, the
grey dawn—a zombie's walk of retribution.

I hold their hands and listen. Keep the book open and
speak.

And prayer begins to work.

God is in the cookies, in the sweet perfume, and shrill
laughter.

The grieving never stops, just moves along the row like a
box of passed tissues.

They create me from nothing to a dancing soul. Amend
me, change me, confirm me, so I can see that dead glove is
just some white-trash joke, and not a message left for me.

Hallelujah.

God Dishes

I do worship you. How could I not? When yesterday my
hands were hot in sudsy water, cleaning the guck from
dishes, I prayed to you.
My selfishness overwhelmed me with angry pride and as I
scrubbed I prayed, release me like a dargnabble stuck to a
scuzzy cup.

And within minutes I read a message sent from you? A
breathtaking blossom of your love and I stared
disbelieving you could be so swift, so direct as running
water, rinsing away my doubt.

Restoration to Sanity

Before the survival sisters took over, twelve strong and brilliant beings stood in my ready soul. Restoration is to a time before fear and want, to truth and purpose, linking arms in glorious pursuit of a life worth living.

How far we angels fall – the swirling dizzying descent through arms of men and spirit bottles, hard, hard feelings, bitter and desperate, to a damned crash landing of disbelief and ego.

And the survival sisters walk and talk and clothe me — sell each other on the street, spend the money feeding starving jukeboxes, turn endless frightened cheeks, and shamed, crawl and pull the curtains down, dump piss from windows high above the parade.

Restoration – a slow recognition, a glimmer from the basement, a bare bulb burning. The slow wreckage and stripping – the trash piling up outside – ticked mattresses with sordid stains and mouldy plaster drunk and stinking lathe and mice nests, 1960s linoleum and a heating system still spitting and breathing hot dry nothingness.

Everything new, in its original place, ordered by divine design and fitted with dove tail joints, a supple hand, perfect, solid and apt. And I walk through. The floor boards creak in all the right places, the lights switch on, the cupboards close effortlessly. The stairs lead up where I am sleeping sanely during night time hours. There is food in the fridge, the clock is cuckooing, everything is in place and I start humming.

Lost Dog

On days I dare to love I am lifted and float, one hand on a
worn bench, one eye on a flying wasp, the wind lifting my
crazy hair as I listen to an autistic boy speak earnestly into
a camera.
Tears spring. I am grateful. I am grateful. On days like
these, there is an absence.

My desire to demolish and push the mistaken ones away
clouds and colours me, a lava dark stony black and I cool
and the sun cannot find me and I crawl on those days. I
forget. I lose my self like a dog lost on the sand.

Air Show

Just wanted to say, on this fine dull morning, how yesterday you sat at a picnic table grinning at me from a face I'd never seen. And you reached out and into me and expelled an obsession taxiing there for takeoff.

My ears are open, not full of sand or pain. Open to hear the wind and the rumbling thunder of a stealth bomber. I look up and see a gull gliding, and a kite flying. And all that sound, all that noise, is in my head.

Your kindness flies like sand over my feet, like music and swaying hips, like laughter on my lips. And I hear you and feel you. The comfort as big as the sky, as opaque as this overcast day.

Artichoke

I replace a word in my affirmation. I pluck hope like an
olive from the jar and drop in trust – the intentional
artichoke.
I had a futile hope for love. I hoped it would jab him. But
hope is just an insipid prayer – my hopes crash and flee
like spilt pearl onions across the floor. But trust, I strain to
pry the lid from. Trust. I was a fool again. Trust, so prickly
and elusive, sticks tickly in my throat.
I lick my fingers, taste vinegar there, savour trust, a
flavour unfamiliar.

Fishing

I'm fishing in a fathomless pond, reeling in six today, no
seven, piscine quicksilver, so easily forgotten, dragged
from depths below I remember.
The water tranquil, mere ripples across the deep dark
green, a verdant vast pool of whispers and secrets. I pull
them gasping for life, breathe into them, they don't die,
dancing in the pail, spider web tails. I write their weight
and tip it, escape, to be caught again.

At the fish & chip shop, I watch the greasy cook smoking
in the kitchen. Something sizzles. The pimply limp girl
says, "That'll be fourteen ninety-five." And I believe her.

Anticipate Nothing

I plan this moon in vain attempt to control the nonexistent
pain which threatens, in reminder, to overwhelm me
again, and spend Friday night on a beached log with you
watching it at ninety-seven percent.
Dancing on the still water of Lake Ontario, its ascent
picturesque and inconsequent, our sandaled feet snuggled
into cool night sand as little boys in baseball caps descend
and your blackberry buzzes as you describe to me your
pop top and your Beatle boots and the creep who tried to
lure you with his bad intent.
I laugh so hard my menopausal bladder squawks and you
delight me staggering drunken (without a drop) in revelry
down the moonlit boardwalk.

And on one hundred percent night, it hides behind the
clouds. The moon painless this year, rather, an exquisite
joy for all the glittering on the lake, the pull 'tween you
and me – the turning tide.

The End

INDEX

A Dead and Dying Dog, 29
A Friend with Skin, 43
Abuse, 48
Air Show, 111
And Deliver Us from Evil, 78
Anticipate Nothing, 114
Artichoke, 112
Baby Zombie, 2
Bad Timing*, 57
Balls, 66
Barn Fire, 65
Birds on a Roof, 64
Blameless, 45
Blooms, 54
Business, 28
Caged, 61
Candy Man, 60
Chattering, 1
Chicken, 76
Choices, 33
Cinderella, 8
Clementine, 53
Close, 74
Coming and Going, 50
Concupiscence, 63
Cracker Jack, 83
Creamsicle, 58
Croatia, 7
Crucible, 93
Dead Horse, 40
Divorcée, 41
Eden, 49

Erato, 87
Eros Ascending: A Book Review, 101
Exit, 82
February Days, 21
Fingers, 42
Fishing, 113
Flock of Crows, 13
Fracture, 16
Free, 39
Full Moon Coming, 32
Garbage Day, 26
God Dishes, 108
Goodbye, 86
Grief Poems, 14
Hansel, 12
Hello Winter, 18
Hidden, 106
Honey from the Rock, 72
Hostage, 10
iPod, 5
Knock, 96
Last Days, 25
Last Whisker, 42
Little Prince, 55
Lost Dog, 110
Maybe, 70
Mercy, 4
More, 102
Never, 24
Not Listening, 37
Not Listening Again, 27
Nourishment, 9
Old Goat, 81
Pig, 89

Pillow, 85
Pressure, 68
Red Light, 92
Resentment Doll, 17
Resolution, 51
Restoration to Sanity, 109
Rockabye, 47
Salt & Pepper, 59
Shallow End, 30
Shh, 71
Silence, 19
Silent Treatment, 36
Since I Met You, 98
Sinners, 104
Snap Dragon, 77
Snap Shot, 3
Spellbound, 79
Spilt Ink, 88
Spinning, 6
St. Valentine's Day, 23
Status Quo, 52
Suffering, 103
Summarizing, 34
Sun, 99
Surgery, 90
Tea Bag, 38
Temple of God, 95
The Apple Tree, 56
The Daisy, 69
The Dam, 44
The Difference, 100
The Lyric in You, 62
The Meeting Place, 107
The Punishment, 37

The Witch, 11
Time, 105
To the Archer, 67
Trees, 22
Undertow, 31
Voyeur, 75
Wasted, 91
Words, 20
Worm, 35
Yes, 97

ACKNOWLEDGEMENTS

"Summarized" appeared May 12, 2011 www.SeaGiraffe.com
"Chattering" appeared June 3, 2011 www.snakeoilcure.com
"Undertow" appeared April 5, 2011 www.snakeoilcure.com

Throughout my life I've had wonderful poetry teachers —
thank you Brian Bailey, John Hughes,
Janet Williams, and bp Nichol.
Thanks to my lifelong readers,
especially Stephen DeGange, and Nancy Day.
Thanks to Patrick Ballantyne for the shove off the cliff.
Thanks to Tom Hamilton for the boost of courage.
Thanks to Kelly Greer for the mirror.
And to all my friends and family for reading
and loving me, thank you.

Also by Sandy Day . . .

Excerpt from

Fred's Funeral

CHAPTER ONE

It is thin and wavering, the barrier Fred Sadler knocks against. But no matter how hard he tries, he cannot pass through. He is like timber in a lake, submerged and waterlogged and the boys above him are gulls in the sky. Fred Sadler doesn't know he is in that disagreeable place—reserved for those who predetermine there is no life after death but who, upon dying, discover indeed there is more.

It's the damnedest thing. Fred Sadler waves and calls out to his cousin Birdie and his brother Thomas as the two boys beckon him closer. They are youngsters, just how Fred Sadler remembers them and he longs to be with them. Behind Birdie and Thomas, a strange grove of glorious verdant trees glows and sways. Beyond the trees, Fred glimpses the pure blue brilliance of water. The two boys peer toward Fred Sadler and Thomas asks Birdie, "Is it Fred? Can he not cross over?"

Fred tries again to penetrate the misty layer but he's held back. Something whispers, As through a glass darkly.

Fred hears the voice of a long ago Congregationalist Church minister breaking through his consciousness like a radio suddenly tuned into a station. When I was a child, I spoke as a child, I understood as a child, I thought as a child; but when I became a man, I put away childish things.

What in the blue deuce?

On the other side of the ethereal boundary, Fred's whole family is congregating, all the people who died and went on before him. All the souls he'd felt certain he would never see again. There's Fred's mother wearing the look of sweet worry she'd borne after the war, and there's his father—so proud of Fred, and Pauline, lovely lithe Pauline, laughing and twirling, and by gum there's Fred's old friend Stanley!

Hello, hello!

A noise below startles Fred Sadler and he realizes with a jolt that it is October 12, 1986 and he is floating near the pocked beige ceiling of his room in York Manor Home for the Aged. Inches from his nose is that horrid brown stain from the flood in the bathroom upstairs – it's unmistakable—he's spent years lying on his back studying it.

Am I dead?

Fred Sadler thrashes, trying to locate his brother and family and the lush green world but it's vanished. Dammit! Where did that dream go? They are expecting me. I want to go back!

Below him, Fred's sister-in-law Viola, and her son John are opening a black leather suitcase on Fred's rumpled and recently vacated cot. A sickly sweet waft rises from the suitcase reaching Fred's being up by the ceiling. Until this moment, Fred Sadler had quite forgotten about the battered old suitcase stored in the basement of the nursing home. He realizes now that storage had been unnecessary, it's not as though anyone ever checked out from York Manor alive. The suitcase is wider than the bed and the pink ribbons that once held it agape have rotted through. Fred's nephew, John props the lid against the wall.

Viola holds a gloved hand over her nose and mouth. "Good gracious. What's he kept in there?" She stands a little to the side and watches as John inspects the contents.

"Nothing of value," she sniffs. And then adds, "We are not taking that home."

I should hope not! Fred Sadler whirls over the bed incensed at the interruption of his heavenly reverie with Thomas and Birdie and the lovely others. Why, Viola hasn't visited him since before his brother Thomas died, not that Fred had wanted to see her. Damn you, old woman!

Viola surveys the contents of the suitcase. She hesitates before reaching in gingerly and removing the lid from a two-pound Laura Secord chocolate box nestled on the top of some papers. It aggravates Fred Sadler, no end to see Viola monkeying around with his things but there doesn't seem to be anything he can do to prevent her. He is dead. He swirls around the small room in agitated circles.

In the candy box is a smaller velvet box containing Fred's two wartime medals.

Hands off!

One medal, on an orange and blue ribbon, says in capital letters, THE GREAT WAR FOR CIVILISATION 1914 – 1919. On the back is an angel in a boastful pose holding a long feather or frond gesturing toward who knows what. The other medal, on a rainbow-striped ribbon, depicts a mounted horse stomping on a shield; a tiny sun shines over the horse's head; in the foreground a skull and crossbones lies. A grim scene. The medal says, 1914 – 1918. On the back is the bearded profile of King George V. The ribbons are mixed up – they're on the wrong medals. Fred Sadler remembers he used to like to fiddle with them—Viola will probably notice and think he's daft.

"Uncle Fred's medals?" John asks.

Viola snaps the velvet lid shut. "Everybody got those," she says. "Everybody that came home, that is." She pauses. "Don't you remember the newsreels, John?"

"Mom. I wasn't even born until World War II."

"Well, there were newsreels then too."

John sighs.

"You know, two of my cousins didn't come home from the war," Viola continues.

John nods.

"They died in training accidents right before the end."

"I remember you telling me."

Viola passes the candy box to John who picks out a pair of spurs, the brown leather straps stiff and crackled but still intact. Only one jagged wheel, for digging into the horse's flank, is still attached and twirlable, the other no doubt lies under a field of poppies somewhere in Flanders. It hadn't come home with Fred, he remembers that.

"When did Uncle Fred ever ride a horse?" John asks.

"Everybody rode horses in those days," Viola scoffs.

John examines the tarnished silver porridge spoon an eighteen-year-old Fred had plucked from his mother's silverware drawer on his way to encampment seventy years earlier, a spoon that had resided in Fred's boot next to his shin as he'd trudged the short and endless miles from Ypres to Amiens and back again. The sight of the spoon makes Fred Sadler wistful as hell. Suddenly he feels the urge to tell the story of the dreadful meals taken with that spoon, the billycans and trench dinners, the cold milky tea it had stirred.

In the wobbly globes that used to be Fred Sadler's eyes, a rush of clear cold tears surges. It occurs to Fred Sadler, in uncharacteristic sentimentality, that long ago he'd passed up the opportunity, when John was a lad, his brother's child, his only nephew, to have a relationship with the boy, this man John; to hear him call him Uncle; to sit with him on his knee and tell him war stories, or take him fishing on Lake Simcoe. Fred's brother Thomas, the child version, flashes again in front of Fred Sadler, laughing and calling—and then he's gone again before Fred can grasp him. This dying business is mucking me up.

John tosses the spoon back into the box with a clang. "Kind of an odd thing to hang onto."

Fred Sadler remembers now why he always disliked John. The child had avoided him, called him weird Uncle Fred. He'd heard John whispering to his sisters, "Shhh, he's got shell shock." But it was young John who was the holy terror—running and tripping, scraping his knees, knocking his teeth out, jumping off the swing and breaking his arms, and the noise that issued from the child. When he wasn't buzzing like an aeroplane or berserk with laughter, he was bleating like a homeless sheep or whining like a hinge. Fred couldn't bear being in the same room with John, or any of those children.

Viola pokes about in the contents on the bottom of the Laura Secord box—the brass buttons and pins from Fred's old uniform. As she snoops, a corporeal fury courses through Fred Sadler's being. The sensation startles Fred and he looks down at what he can only refer to as his self, his now legless and somewhat opaque form. Though still a shadowy version of the frail ninety-year-old chest and arms he sported the day before, he is now wearing his scratchy and faded old Canadian Expeditionary Force uniform from 1916. The jacket is ghostly — the empty buttonholes sewn up like sleeping eyes.

John fingers a brass maple leaf in the bottom of the box. "What is all this stuff?"

"I have no idea," Viola answers.

It's the damnedest thing. Fred Sadler has not allowed himself to think about the past for a very long time, but now he remembers the day his brother Thomas had arrived with the Laura Secord box in his hands. It was way back in the asylum, in Whitby. It must have been the 1960s, before Thomas finally moved Fred to York Manor.

www.sandyday.ca

Printed in Poland
by Amazon Fulfillment
Poland Sp. z o.o., Wrocław